Searchlight BOOKS™

Discover Planets

W9-AMA-845

Discover

Mercury

Georgia Beth

Lerner Publications ◆ Minneapolis

Lerner Publications Company
A division of Lerner Publishing Group, Inc.
241 First Avenue North
Minneapolis, MN 55401 USA

For reading levels and more information, look up this title
at www.lernerbooks.com.

Main body text set in Adrianna Regular 14/20.
Typeface provided by Chank.

Library of Congress Cataloging-in-Publication Data

Names: Beth, Georgia, author.
Title: Discover Mercury / Georgia Beth.
Description: Minneapolis : Lerner Publications, [2018] | Series: Searchlight books.
    Discover planets | Audience: Ages 8–11. | Audience: Grades 4 to 6. | Includes
    bibliographical references and index.
Identifiers: LCCN 2017058426 (print) | LCCN 2017050334 (ebook) |
    ISBN 9781541525443 (eb pdf) | ISBN 9781541523364 (lb : alk. paper) |
    ISBN 9781541527874 (pb : alk. paper)
Subjects: LCSH: Mercury (Planet)—Exploration—Juvenile literature. | Mercury (Planet)—
    Juvenile literature.
Classification: LCC QB611 (print) | LCC QB611 .B475 2018 (ebook) | DDC 523.41—dc23

LC record available at https://lccn.loc.gov/2017058426

Manufactured in the United States of America
1-44409-34668-1/29/2018

Contents

Chapter 1

MYSTERIOUS MERCURY

The sun dominates the solar system so much that it's easy to ignore the worlds around it. But what lies in its shadow? A planet lurks, one that's both a neighbor and a mystery. Turn your gaze past the sun's bright light. There you'll find Mercury, one of the solar system's least understood places.

Mercury is the smallest planet in the solar system.

MERCURY LOOKS LIKE A SMALL DOT WHEN IT'S VIEWED IN FRONT OF THE SUN.

A Stranger in the Sky

Ancient Sumerians tracked Mercury's movement. Modern scientists studied it to try to prove complex theories about gravity. Those who saw early photographs thought Mercury was similar to our moon. But it has proven to be stranger than we imagined. And still little is known about the small planet that is closest to the sun.

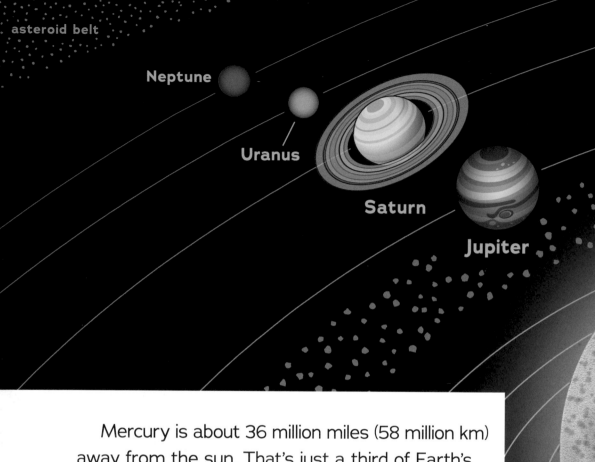

Neptune

Uranus

Saturn

Jupiter

Mercury is about 36 million miles (58 million km) away from the sun. That's just a third of Earth's distance from the sun. And that makes Mercury hard to study. Intense sunlight near the planet can damage telescopes. The sun's strong gravity pulls in space probes. And Mercury's rocky surface doesn't offer any cushion for probes that might try to land there.

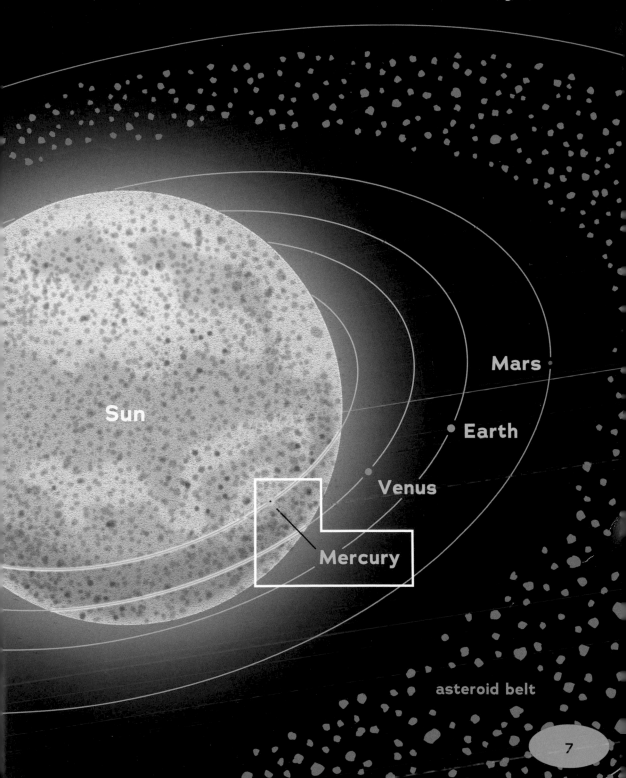

The Solar System

Mars

Earth

Sun

Venus

Mercury

asteroid belt

STEM Highlight

Mercury is the closest planet to the sun. But Venus, which is twice as far from the sun, is hotter. Why? The answer lies in the two planets' atmospheres. Mercury has a very thin atmosphere. But Venus is covered in a thick layer of gas that absorbs and traps the sun's energy, making this distant planet hotter than Mercury.

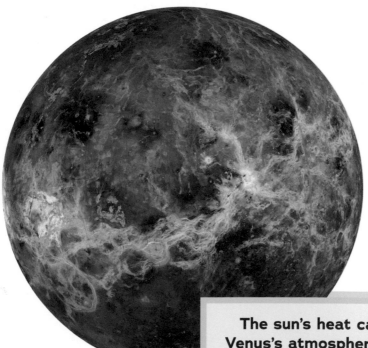

The sun's heat can enter Venus's atmosphere, but the heat can't escape through the thick layer of gases.

Chapter 2

INTENSE AND DENSE

Mercury is a terrestrial planet. That means it shares something in common with Earth. And just like Earth, Mercury's surface is hard. But the similarities stop there.

All but a trace of Mercury's atmosphere has been burned away by the sun. So it would be impossible for humans to breathe on Mercury. This makes it a tough place for life to survive.

In the sky, Mercury (*lower right*) can be seen with the naked eye as a small, glowing dot.

Standing on the surface of Mercury would be nothing like standing on the surface of Earth. The lack of atmosphere on Mercury means everything appears very clear. Without air to filter the sun's light, the sky always looks black. And the stars don't twinkle.

Temperatures on Mercury would be deadly for humans, getting as high as 800°F (427°C) and as low as -290°F (-179°C).

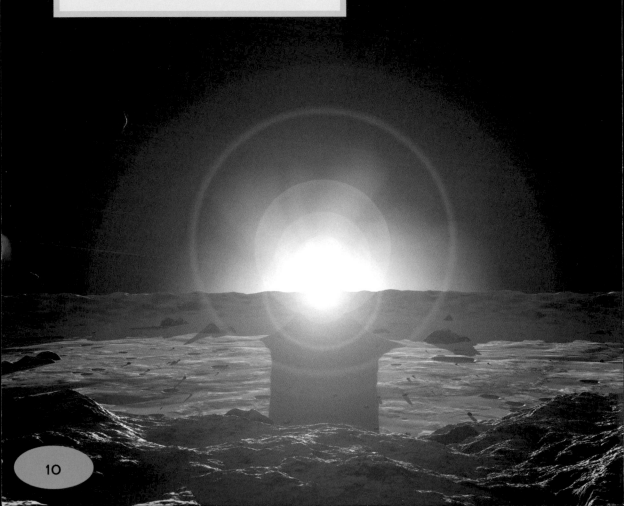

There's no water or lava on Mercury. But asteroids are pummeling the planet. So the ground is covered with craters, dust, and deep hills and valleys. There may also be earthquakes.

There aren't any moons to admire on this planet. But plenty of other things would make you gasp. Since Mercury is close to the sun, it feels the sun's gravity strongly. That causes it to travel around the sun more quickly than any other planet. A year on Mercury is just eighty-eight Earth days long.

Gravity is weaker on Mercury's surface than it is on Earth, so astronauts might be able to leap three times higher on Mercury.

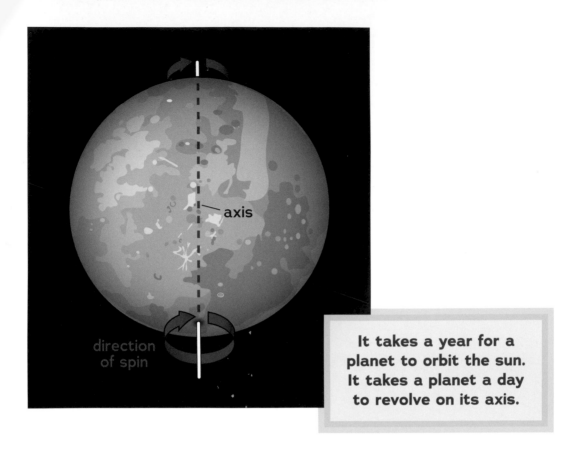

axis

direction
of spin

It takes a year for a
planet to orbit the sun.
It takes a planet a day
to revolve on its axis.

While the years on Mercury are short, the days are long. That's because Mercury rotates on its axis slowly. So a single day on Mercury stretches to nearly fifty-nine Earth days. If you stood in just the right place on Mercury, you could watch a sunrise different from any you've ever seen before! First, you would see the sun rise. But then, it would appear to slow, stop, and set. And then, it would rise again. Since you would be standing so close, the sun would appear to be nearly three times bigger than it looks on Earth!

STEM Highlight

The smallest planet in the solar system may be shrinking! Have you ever seen a big fluffy cookie crinkle and wrinkle as it cools? The same thing appears to be happening to Mercury. When the planet first formed, it was a molten mess. As the core cooled over billions of years, the planet's outer layer crumpled. Scientists think the core is still very hot and active. And the way the outer, cooler layers are shifting is causing the planet to shrink.

In the last four billion years, Mercury has lost 8.6 miles (14 km) in width!

Deeper Layers

What lies under the surface of Mercury? Without exploring more, we can't know for sure. But scientists think the core is large and dense. Mercury's core is made of mostly iron.

Research suggests Mercury's core makes up 61 percent of the planet.

solid core

mantle

crust

Chapter 3

STUDYING THE PLANET

It takes about five minutes for signals from Mercury to reach Earth. But that hasn't stopped scientists from sending probes there. Astronomers have been studying the planet for hundreds of years. No one person discovered the planet. Astronomers saw it in the sky for ages.

Mercury is so close to the sun that the planet isn't always visible from Earth.

WHEN SOMETHING WAXES, IT APPEARS TO GROW BIGGER. WHEN SOMETHING WANES, IT APPEARS TO GROW SMALLER.

One of the first astronomers to study Mercury with a telescope was Giovanni Zupi. In 1639, Zupi found that the planet goes through phases. Just like our moon, it waxes and wanes. This knowledge helped astronomers understand that Mercury orbits the sun and not Earth. That's not news today. But then, it was still debated. Most people thought everything in the universe revolved around Earth. Now we know we're living on a planet that's just one of billions.

A Recent Look

In the 1970s, the US National Aeronautics and Space Administration (NASA) sent *Mariner 10* to visit Venus and Mercury. *Mariner 10* flew past Mercury three times. NASA lost contact with the probe in 1975. But before that, the probe was able to map nearly half the surface of the planet. So many places in the solar system have surprised us. It was likely Mercury would be the same.

Mariner 10 had solar panels, cameras, and other advanced tools to help it explore Venus and Mercury.

The probe sent back images of Mercury's surface. It found a thin layer of helium around the planet. Helium is an odorless, tasteless, colorless gas. The probe also discovered the planet has a small magnetic field. This led scientists to think the metal in the core is not totally solid.

Mercury is a world of extremes. The side facing the sun is incredibly hot, while the other side is frozen. It also has the most elliptical orbit of any planet. Instead of making an even circle around the sun, Mercury's orbit is shaped more like an oval. Mercury spins 28 to 43 million miles (45 to 69 million km) from the sun.

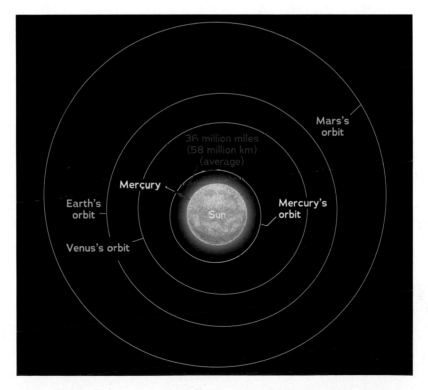

Mars's orbit

36 million miles
(58 million km)
(average)

Mercury

Earth's orbit

Sun

Mercury's orbit

Venus's orbit

Chapter 4

MODERN MISSIONS

In 2011, the *Messenger* probe began orbiting Mercury. Images revealed craters and broad plains. The large cracks and wrinkles covering the plains are called *rupes*, or cliffs. *Messenger* also found ash that showed the planet was home to active volcanoes for at least a billion years.

One volcano on Mercury is larger than the state of Delaware!

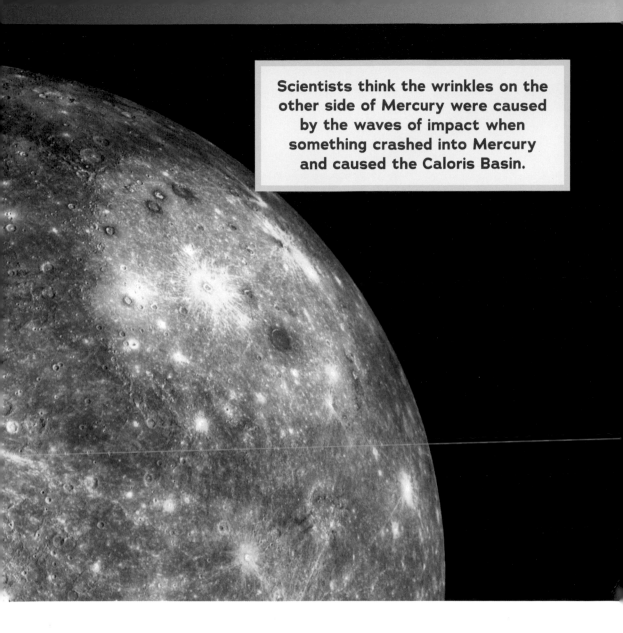

Scientists think the wrinkles on the other side of Mercury were caused by the waves of impact when something crashed into Mercury and caused the Caloris Basin.

Messenger studied the Caloris Basin, a desert 960 miles (1,545 km) across. Data showed the impact that created the basin was so intense that it affected the other side of the planet. The side of the planet exactly opposite from the Caloris Basin is hilly and wrinkled.

Mercury orbits the sun very quickly. So comets and asteroids collide with the planet at higher combined speeds. That causes bigger explosions and bigger craters. These dramatic craters are named after writers and other creative people.

One crater is named Tolkien after *The Hobbit* and *The Lord of the Rings* author J. R. R. Tolkien.

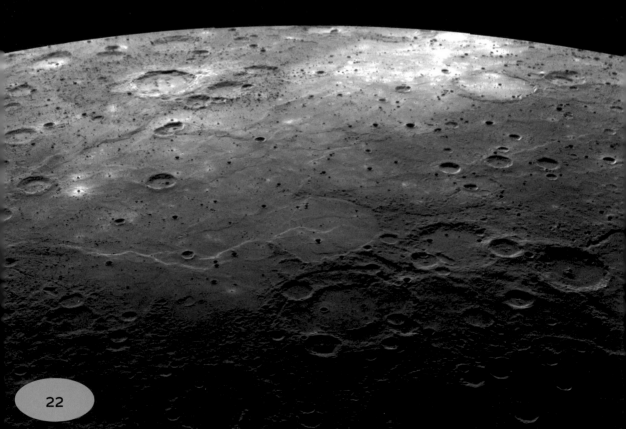

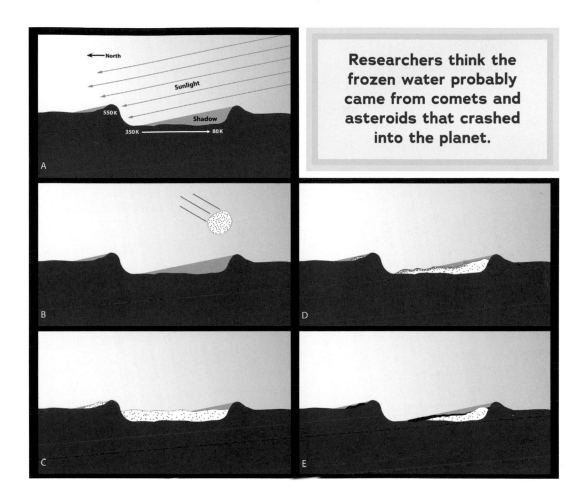

This rocky planet offers more than just rock. Over 100 billion tons (91 billion t) of frozen water lies deep in the craters near the planet's poles. In the craters, temperatures are always below -250°F (-157°C). Sunlight never hits these cold places, so the ice won't be melting into liquid water anytime soon.

RESEARCHERS HOPE TO LEARN MORE INFORMATION ABOUT THESE HOLLOWS.

Volcanoes. Craters. Ice. Mercury has surprised scientists many times, but these features feel a bit familiar. We have similar places on Earth. But *Messenger* also found areas that scientists call hollows. These are flat, irregular shapes, roughly 100 feet (30 m) deep in the ground. There aren't very many craters in these hollows. So it's likely they were made fairly recently. They're made of something mysterious and bright. That's about all scientists know about them.

A Glorious Exit

Scientists designed *Messenger* to orbit for just one year. But they were able to conserve fuel, so it could send back data for three more years. *Messenger* orbited around Mercury 4,105 times. In 2015, *Messenger* finally slammed into the planet. It sent back one last amazing collection of data—and created one more crater.

Messenger's 2015 crash happened on the far side of Mercury, so no one on Earth was able to see it.

Scientists added color to help them study these photos of Mercury taken by *Messenger*.

Data from *Messenger* is still being studied. The mission made people more curious about Mercury. From here on Earth, it simply looks like a light in the sky. But closer up, much more is revealed. *Messenger* showed that Mercury is not just a ball of rock and metal. It's a complex world worth exploring.

Secrets in the Sky

There's still so much we don't understand about Mercury. Studying it will help us understand the solar system and our place in it. Yet this strange world is truly alien. We've been studying it for hundreds of years. And still, we have more questions than answers. This is Mercury's magic. Close and yet mysterious. Dead and yet dynamic. What secrets will be revealed next?

Only time—and more exploration—can tell!

We learn more about Mercury with each research trip. Who knows what we'll learn about it next?

STEM Highlight

Messenger discovered that solar wind from the sun causes storms across Mercury. The winds create leaks and twists in the invisible magnetic field that surrounds Mercury. It's the same kind of magnetic field found around the magnets that stick to refrigerators but much larger. The solar wind has its own magnetic field. Where the solar wind's magnetic field clashes with Mercury's, it causes invisible tornadoes. Scientists think these clashes add to the thin atmosphere found on Mercury.

Looking Ahead

- In 2025, a new probe is scheduled to reach Mercury in a joint mission called BepiColombo. It is a project between the European Space Agency (ESA) and the Japan Aerospace Exploration Agency (JAXA). BepiColombo will look for ice and help scientists understand why the planet is shrinking.

- What may have been the first meteorites from Mercury were found on Earth in 2013. The green rocks, discovered in Morocco, are unlike anything scientists have ever seen before. Scientists are still studying the meteorites to learn more!

- It's impossible to know if people will get to visit Mercury one day. But if they do, they may be happy they can't breathe on the planet! Mercury is covered with more sulfur than any other terrestrial planet. Sulfur smells like rotten eggs.

Glossary

atmosphere: the gases that surround a planet

axis: an invisible line a planet rotates around

core: the central part of a planet

dense: heavier than most things of the same size

dynamic: constantly changing

elliptical: shaped like an oval

gravity: the attraction of the mass of one object to another

helium: a light, colorless gas that does not burn. Helium is used to fill airships and balloons.

magnetic field: the area near a body that carries an electric current that creates magnetic forces

molten: melted at a high temperature, usually describing metal or rock

probe: a device that travels in outer space and collects information

solar system: a group consisting of a star and the planets and other objects that orbit the star. In our solar system, the star is called the sun.

terrestrial planet: a planet that is related to Earth

Learn More about Mercury

Books

Holland, Simon. *Space.* New York: DK, 2016. Filled with images from NASA and research from the Smithsonian, this visual encyclopedia will get you excited about every planet in the solar system.

Kops, Deborah. *Exploring Space Robots.* Minneapolis: Lerner Publications, 2012. Learn how robots can help us explore the solar system.

Squire, Ann O. *Planet Mercury.* New York: Children's Press, 2014. Read this book to find a timeline of the planet and look at what Mercury is made of.

Websites

Mission to Mercury
https://kids.nationalgeographic.com/explore/space/mission-to
-mercury/#mercury-planet.jpg
Learn more about Mercury, and imagine you're on your own mission to explore the planet.

Weather in Space (the Rocky Planets)
https://www.youtube.com/watch?v=Dvhl891zGqU
Watch this video to learn more about the weather on Mercury and other terrestrial planets in our solar system.

What Is the Planet Mercury?
https://www.nasa.gov/audience/forstudents/k-4/stories/nasa-knows
/what-is-planet-mercury-k4.html
Visit this site to learn more information about Mercury and future research plans.

Index

Photo Acknowledgments

The images in this book are used with the permission of: NASA/Johns Hopkins University Applied Physics Laboratory/Carnegie Institution of Washington, pp. 4, 13, 20, 21, 24, 25, 26, 27; NASA/Bill Ingalls, p. 5; © Laura Westlund/Independent Picture Service, pp. 6–7, 12, 14, 19; NASA/JPL, pp. 8, 18; Alan Dyer/VW PICS/UIG/Getty Images, p. 9; Stocktrek Images/Getty Images, p. 10; Detlev van Ravenswaay/Science Source, p. 11; ESO/Y. Beletsky, p. 15; QAI Publishing/UIG/Getty Images, p. 17; NASA, JHU APL, CIW, p. 22; NASA/Johns Hopkins University Applied Physics Laboratory/Carnegie Institution of Washington, p. 23; ESA/NASA/SOHO, p. 28.

Cover: NASA, JHU APL, CIW.